A Sea in the Desert

A Sea in the Desert

Leslie Norris

SEREN BOOKS
*1989

SEREN BOOKS is the book imprint of
Poetry Wales Press Ltd
Andmar House, Tondu Road, Bridgend,
Mid Glamorgan

British Library Cataloguing in Publication Data

Norris, Leslie, *1921-*
    A sea in the desert.
    I. Title
    821'.914

    ISBN 1-85411-015-2

*The publisher acknowledges the financial support of the
Welsh Arts Council*

*The publisher acknowledges the financial support of the
Welsh Arts Council*

Typeset in 11 point Palatino by Megaron, Cardiff
Printed by John Penry Press, Swansea

Contents

I
THE HAWK'S EYE

II
THE DARK MONTHS

III
STONES TREES WATER

Acknowledgements

These poems have appeared in *The New Yorker*, *Atlantic Monthly*, *London Magazine*, *London Review of Books*, *New Criterion*, *Tar River Poetry*, *Poetry Wales*, *Planet*, *Fine Madness*, *Literature and Belief*, and *Hubbub*.

Excerpts from 'Stones Trees Water' were published as *A Tree Sequence* by the Sea Pen Press, Seattle. The whole sequence of forty-one poems was broadcast by the B.B.C.

For my brothers,
Eric and Gordon

I

THE HAWK'S EYE

THE HAWK'S EYE

for Fred Ewoldt

The hawk carries his eye
out of swinging altitudes
higher than winter.
Above his locked feet,
hunched in wet feathers,
he rages in larches.
It is the snow brings him down.

Bland snow has covered
the rock of the precipice.
Is the hawk to hang
above so changed a world?
He knows the quiet architecture
of high places, the black
argument of granite.

But the snow's in his eye
and he shrieks in temper.
I could use that harsh gaze
above the crested summit
of fluted snow, and the curved
stretches of ledges.
I could look down

between the grasp of my arms
on the still air
and see in the dark
the stars of dark farms
in the huddle of winter,
their byres shut to the night
and their eyes turned to the fire.

I could see the men
I might have become
turn out of their stiff clothes
to sleep the cold night, fatigued,
under heavy blankets
woven by their mothers.
I could see a man,

perturbed, hearing foxes bark,
move with his lantern
across the muffled yard
into his barn
where the spent chaff,
light, lighter than air,
will rise in his little flame,

climb in the small heat,
motes, thin dust of old harvests,
until the man turns,
grumbling at the cold,
thumbs shut his latch
against the high snow
where the hawk is at watch.

THESE HILLS, THESE WOODS

Who comes out of these hills, these woods,
from the small white house in the hollow,
from the summer river between ferns?
Who travels the rough lanes worn

by the stumbling dung-cart? They carry
among the bundled clutter of clothes and pans
and the rattle of what is portable
the whole of their lives. That one,

larky, long in the leg, red-bearded, he
will not come back. Already his grave
is marked, he will not see his grandchildren.
The young one, who knows the flight

of lark and pipit and holds their bald nestlings
within his hands, will fall apprentice
to a butcher. He will run screaming
from the slaughterhouse, his eyes full

of hacked red meat, the round cries
of animals will follow him all his roads.
He will walk through the dark lots,
through brutal labour in furnaces,

through human betrayal. His sisters
will curb their thin tongues, laugh
bitterly and in secret; endure. They will
never return. It is I who recall their ghosts

to the house lost under the hill, their
wavering dust so frail it does not stir
the powder of the roads. It is I
who people the lanes of homecoming

and build the fallen chimneys stone by stone
so the doused fires will carry the echoes
of old warmth, and the fields hear more
than the hawk's voice, and the silence after.

HAWK MUSIC

At this height I have to say
there are no boundaries
but those of river and bluff.

This eye ignores
the political world,
is concerned with what's visible.

Its happiness is to watch
the intricate valleys weathering
and the wearing down

of upturned faces of rock.
Let me lean into this wind,
so rare that its demands

are those of music. I would
give it a note on the thinnest
string of air, a sound

so high the ear cannot
support it. But I
will hope to hear it.

THE SUMMER HAWK

I wait in blue light, for
early thermals, a hint
of lift. My arms stretch

in effortless recognition, in
widening order at the day's turn.
Counties are opening under me,

in daylight, for my regard;
their fields, sleeping houses
beneath their tiles. The sun's

on my back, the cross of my shadow
closes a wood of singers.
One tractor hangs the pale

of its exhaust against a hedge.
I begin to organize my patterns,
shadows that lean into darkness,

anglers tied to their water all down
the river. And in the meadows
cruel children hunt among flowers.

A DYING HAWK

She stoops and drops
through a straight
funnel of sight
into falling air.
She folds gravity
to her heart, and dives

behind her eye.
The one purpose
of her gaze
will not let her see
the clear windscreen
moving to kill her.

She spreads too late.
Her wings, her talons
set against air.
She dies at the roadside,
her hollow bones
are splintered

in the rags of her feathers,
and her brittle gape
is open and broken.
Before her head falls
what is left
stares from her yellow eye.

THE HAWK MAPS HIS COUNTRY

The rivers crawl to the sea.
I bring them down
through gullies of rain,
flatten them in valleys
slide their silver estuaries
into darker water.
Gulls ride the ripples,
svelte waterbirds, breathers
of a thicker air. Kittiwakes,
snickering herring gulls,
and in the reeds, white,
white as a pearl,
a single ivory gull,
eater of excrement.

A populace of shorebirds
struts the yellow ledge
between land and water.
Stilts, knots, sharp snipe,
phalaropes in their variety,
avocets and sandpipers,
let them wade and preen,
petty turnstones,
community birds.

Flocks of goldeneyes
occupy the water,
mergansers, eiders,
a flight of cinnamon teal,
stiff-tailed, red.
Let them glow

in their common element,
and on domestic ponds
let Aylesburys paddle.

In a change of weather
the wild geese
fly their wide arrows
over my ranges,
yelping at night
as they pass under the moon,
a compass in their skulls.
I will not stop their lanes.
The seasons follow them.
They draw the sun behind them,
birds of the tender meadows,
oiled against moisture.

My eye measures
the edges of the world.
I am centre and rim
of its only soaring.
I hold the high Sierras
in the grip of my claws.
I call, and it is my voice
answers. When at last
I tumble headlong
out of serene wheeling
I shall leave a cry
hanging beyond echo
in the sustenance of air.
The earth will be heavy
with the puff of my dust.

HUDSON'S GEESE

'...I have, from time to time, related some incident of my boyhood, and these are contained in various chapters in *The Naturalist in La Plata, Birds and Man, Adventures among Birds....*'

W.H. Hudson, in *Far Away and Long Ago.*

Hudson tells us of them,
the two migrating geese,
she hurt in the wing
indomitably walking
the length of a continent,
and he wheeling above,
calling his distress.
They could not have lived.
Already I see her wing
scraped past the bone
as she drags it through rubble.
A fox, maybe, took her
in his snap jaws. And what
would he do, the point
of his circling gone?
The wilderness of his cry
falling through an air
turned instantly to winter
would warn the guns of him.
If a fowler dropped him,
let it have been quick,
pellets hitting brain
and heart so his weight
came down senseless,
and nothing but his body
to enter the dog's mouth.

THE HAWK CLIMBS

The hawk climbs, and climbing,
seems to hang for ever;

but he too passes over the hill.
Once I found a hawk's skull,

dry, stern hook and bone,
not changed for centuries,

perfected. Yet the seasons
took him, for all his mastery.

I look through the hawk's lens
for an essence I guess at,

the place where his circling ends
and nothing turns into the dark.

Mice under the leaves, speckled
pebbles, I can see them; and

the small dust kicked up
by boys running from school.

I can feel hard growing
in the bones of such children.

There's not a movement
in the country of my eyes

which is not counted. But where
are the lean young men who live

for ever? How far are the fields
where broken ponies run, their legs

made whole? Where is that green
country which put an end to time?

Until that land is found
I search with the hawk's eye.

II

THE DARK MONTHS

ISLANDS

for Garold Davis

Summer's first day, earlier
if the sun were hot enough,
someone would think of water.
We'd run to search in cupboards
for our old swimming trunks,
roll them in towels,
and make our way upriver.
We'd pass the thinning houses
at the edge of town,
pass Pulman's cautious house
behind its wall, his raging
mastiff choking in its snarls.
Two fifty-six pound weights
dragged after him, slowed him.
Old Pulman came out sometimes,
shouting his nervous threats,
easing his beast to calm,
wiping the white froth
with his hands
from the dog's jowls.

But we would be long gone,
aimed for a green elbow
of the river, below the bridge,
where quiet water lingered.

In April once, early sun
deceiving us, we found
three taller boys
already in our pool,

hooting with brisk chill,
calling us to join them.
They could all swim,
floated downstream,
churned water, struck out
across the current.
But the tireless river
throughout its seasons
had filed a narrow channel,
deep, carrying hidden water.
It kept us splashing near the bank,
timid on shallow pebbles.

Boysie Wilde carried me across,
my small weight almost sinking him.
But he swam on, head lifted,
gasping, keeping his breath dry.
He set me in another country,
on the far side of danger,
waist deep in a strange river.
Little waves floated me,
bumped me inch by inch
down a stone ledge. I watched
my legs hang pale
in deep water. Later,
grown cold, I pushed away,
thrashed with my arms
above imagined fathoms,
crawled safely out. The kind
of useless daring I was good at.

That was the day Reg Smith,
knowing that Channel swimmers
cover themselves in grease
to still the cold,
brought half a pound of lard
to keep his white skin warm.
And in he stepped, laid his plumpness
in the clean river. At once
the fat slid off, spreading
in frailest rainbows, fled
in films until the broken shallows
took them.

Walking home, glowing,
we were fulfilled.

It was a known world then.
We lived in it, we made it
with our voices. Somewhere,
we had no doubt of it,
there would be islands
in which the temperate sun
allowed for daylong swimming.
In a world like ours
perfect things were probable.

Meanwhile we walked a world
sound to its very core.
Who could have thought
its crust so thin that men
would burn it dry, shatter it?

We did not imagine
our days were counted.

In Africa, Reg Smith, only child
of old parents, his body
wrapped in khaki, burned away
and vanished in his smoke.
With many others, appalled,
confused, all certainty gone.
They did not find the islands.

I have not found the islands,
islands of peace, of the blest;
but would believe in them,
would search for them, would
keep them floating,
with my breath.

AT THE GRAVE OF DYLAN THOMAS

If I were young I could
Make eager grief of this grave
And let the warm sorrow come
And cover me like a wave,
The cathartic tears ease out
That soothe the constricted heart.

It would be over and done —
A romantic memory made
Out of this drift of rain
And the passive part I played.
Spontaneous youth is gone;
The moved heart is a stone.

Time makes a flint of the heart
That grief cannot spark into flame,
A stubborn, intractable weight
Moved but to inadequate blame.
Here, between hill and sea,
Resignation rules finally.

So I'll not denounce this death
Nor embitter the ordinary air
With blown words that my breath
Is now too small to wear.
Sufficient that he is gone;
A great man dies alone.

Headland, river and bay
Wait for the implied night,
And I, as I move away,

Accept a mutinous fate,
Accept the perpetual sea's
Recurrent elegies.

Seabirds adorning the hill
Move with a bickering grace
As each descending bird
Settles into its place.
Smoothly the plain day ends.
Nothing can make amends.

CHRISTMAS IN UTAH

In barns turned from the wind
the quarter-horses
twitch their laundered blankets.
Three Steller's Jays,
crests sharp as ice,
bejewel the pine tree.
Rough cold out of Idaho
bundles irrational tumbleweed
the length of Main Street.

Higher than snowpeaks,
shriller than the frost,
a brazen angel blows his silent trumpet.

THE DARK MONTHS

Frost nails to the soil
the slots of deer.
Snow will cover them
the dark months of the year.

Waxwings strip from the branch
last fleshes of berry —
haw and firethorn nourish
their starving journey.

It is an eternal star
above the high Uintas
offers its untouched light,
its cold promises.

A MESSAGE FOR DAFYDD AP GWILYM

They tell me you were an aristocrat, Dafydd.
There were none in Merthyr Tydfil,

But for the upstart ghosts of the Crawshays
And old Doctor Ward from Victoria Street.

His was the corner house (with orchard)
Whose tumbled masonry lies in the dirty car park.

It took his housemaid three hours to polish
The great brass headlamps of his open tourer,
A Sunbeam, painted white, already vintage,
But very deeply loved, you could see that.

In steep, appalling rain he hoodless drove
From Dowlais Top, the fine stuff of his suit
Turned black with rain, his monocle awash,
The corrugations of his grimace draining water
Off that wild skull. From Rossi's doorway
I saluted him, without irony, intoning loud:

The chair he sat in, like a burnished throne.

Where there's no sense there's no feeling,
Said Tommy Probert, my fruity companion.

But I thought it patrician enough —
In the hour of its need he did not desert his car.
You might have agreed with Tommy Probert.

And once at a luncheon
I sat next to Lord Goodman.

In Cyfarthfa Castle School, reading around the class,
My turn was 'The Solitary Reaper'.
I read it well enough to make the teacher peevish.
You've learned that by heart, he grieved,
To spout at some *eisteddfod*. I agreed.
I had not seen it before, ever.

It's the words, of course, we can't leave them.
These for your ears, from the town's edge:
Pwllywhiaid, Castell Morlais, Caemaridwn.
And these, among the streets, for mine:
Incline Top, The Ballcourt, the Tramroad.

I've written, too. of those
Manifestations of the natural world,
Birchtrees, birdsong, the inconvenient
Snow, so often your concern.
Like you, I am from the south, like you
I had (in youth) the pale hair
You boast of; in youth
I was slender and thin-faced.

For these dubious affinities, Dafydd,
I tell you — though you have no need to ask —
Dafydd, you are not dead, you will not die.

III

STONES TREES WATER

STONES TREES WATER

1

Sticks and stones
are what the tides let fall in haphazard
order; rubbed pebbles nesting in sand,
casual spars and twigs dark with continual
water, lolling in companies. And what
the rivers cast at summer's dry edges,
mark of the burly flood, measure
of the winter course, bleached now,
and quiet. And quiet the slow grating
of rolling surfaces, helpless the soft twigs.
Impervious small round fragments
of mountain, splinters of soaked forest.

2

Walking the round limestone hills, above
the line where chill springs bubble
from stone clefts, we are aware
of the scarce trees. An elm, and
an elm, and at the edge of our sight
three more in a still dance. And no more,
however we may look. Why is it, after
a day's walking on this sweet grass, we see
the rooted trees still with us, an elm,
an elm, and three quiet elms far off,
poised for dancing?

3

Impossible to see the first pale
tendrils, thinner than hair, frail,
diffident, inexorably working the long
seasons for a true grasp of earth.
And ripening in time so that the grown tree,
its whole upright leafing,
is held by the roots' great fist
clamped about rock and cavity,
sleek shoots thickened and hardened.
We do not see the tenuous, early
pluck at the thin skin of the world,
but look now at the admirable
driving power of the rooted beech!

4

What trick of the strengthening
light, what angle of the tilting world
to the sun, what is the alarm
that sets the trees to work?
Solitary in grazed meadows,
or grouped in copse and hanger, trees
ripen their plump buds
at some green signal
of returning spring.

5

The tree is a slow fountain, erupting
inch by inch
from a deep source
it creates for itself.
Balked, it pauses,
gathers its power
to lift away whatever prison
had thought to hold it down;
then moves purely upward, thrown slowly.
The tree spreads wide its elements,
they branch and fall,
subject to gravity;
a spray, a frail drift,
a falling away.

6

A great tree stands in its wide
shade; generous, still trunk.
Its branches, stalks, leaves
hold air and light. I stand
at its broad foot and think
of the rooted strength,
large as a tree, and branched,
wrapped about earth and stone,
grasping the spinning world.

7

Smooth bole of the beech tree, grey
as elephants, but not wrinkled,
it hides with tidy scars the snags
of dropped branches, and holds
to the light its scatterings
of pointed tawny buds and fresh green leaves.
In Slindon Woods, in a cathedral
of high beeches, the perfect one,
standing without shake or bend,
is called 'Beauty'. Someone,
with neat respect, has carved her name
on the mellow bark; and she, indifferent
to the name, has nearly healed it away.

8

In the beech wood, when light
is perfect green, underwater colour,
green of sunlight filtered
through prodigal green leaves, our hands
and upturned paler faces green, our
very walking and talking freshened
by green light —
then,
one branch of one tree, from its smallest
twig inward, changes; and all along
its length is radiant gold. So that we see
more clearly the green.

9

Grown tall, the trees stand
near my door, knock
on my wall. I need them
less for their globed fruit,
generous victoria, russet,
the streaky pippin, than for
the interweaving of their branches,
dark on a dark sky. I watch
their branched involvements
with the wind, and when, too dark
to see, I pull the blind across
their restlessness, my arms
reach upward, fingers
stretch like twigs.

10

Wealth of the beech, its spendthrift
copper pence are thrown in heaps
and drifts on sparse grass. Chaffinches
pick there, neat in their close feathers,
looking for beech nuts. Eddies and currents
of loose gusts blow the leaves. Dry,
tenacious, carried by water, wrecked
on roads and pavements, they do not rot,
are bountiful still in drifts and heaps,
and brave as single medals on the ground.
They see their green heirs swing above them.

11

Green winter sun touches the yearning poplars.
They stretch to it, creak their swaying trunks
in the brisk wind. Do they feel in their bent
terminal branches the stirring of the seasons?
Are the constrictions of the iron ground
painful to them? Momentary clouds
pass over them, their shadows scud
away. And high in the sudden, luminous
blue of the revealed sky, see there, the pale
enigmatic symbol of the daylight moon.

12

There are no simple seasons, sufficient
to themselves. Summer leaves,
swinging in glossy plenty from the boughs,
remind us of the January trees,
black in the cold rain. We tread
the old leaves underfoot,
leaves six months dead. We walk
among the brief generations of leaves
towards winter.

13

Revealed by winter, small trees
stand like rueful old men,
their bare shanks thin, their
old veins hardening. Useless
to promise as we walk among them
a renewal of youth, a returned
flaunting of green,
when April comes.
They are turned now
from the wind
that shaped their growing
and it is enough
that they endure
what each day's weather
brings to them.
And who is so rash
as to promise us
another April?

14

In a bitter night, if the mists
demand, trees are encased
in white dampness, trunk, branch
and twig; and solidifying frost
turns all such trees to glass.
I have seen an orchard of glass,
white as dawn, where I thought
to have found only solid Bramleys.
A whole country can be suspended
in deluding fog. Men, coming out
to their steaming flocks, will hear
trees crack and splinter, fibres
shredding beneath the tiny axe of ice.

15

As it falls, the tree squeals
in its fibres. Heavy, pulling apart
its dry strings, it bounces
once against the earth, and settles.
Chainsaws slice it in coarse
roundels. What is left, brushwood,
torso, splintered ends
of branches, burns for days
in a corner of the field. Smoke
drifts under the hedge. Darkness
uncovers small red stars
flaring in the soft ash.

16

Winter strips the wood. Bones
of snapped bramble litter the hedges.
Pale moths, frail as paper, fall
in the moon from cracks of bark.
I walk in the cold light, hearing
the trees complain from their stiffened branches,
seeing grains of frost stiffen the yellow grass.

17

The stacked logs wait to blaze
to a quick ash their long, bright summers.
Lithe boughs that held the air
in a mesh of leaves, and swung
to the caprice of the free breeze,
are lopped blunt piles now,
for all their annual circles.
Fallen to saws and chopped
in fireside lengths, they dry away
their old sweet Aprils, and shrink
from their harsh, dry bark.

18

Under the hill a shadow
hides all in its small night, tree,
stone, grass cropped short by rabbits.
And it moves to cover, as earth
turns over into darkness, the black
tree, black grass, sleeping fields
turned up to night. Night's breath
is soft as shadows under the hill.

19

Monotonous winds
invade the fields, the empty spaces.
Bleak light reveals the trees,
blunt stumps of trunks, cracked
branches, rubbed, cancerous bark;
old scars of surviving.
We walk the broken wood
as through another war. Winter
rehearses the end of the world.

20

The winter water wears its pure skin,
ablaze with cold light. Tottering
flocks of mallard, their webs
bemused, search for their floating
element; but the water's hard,
is glass and mirror. On banks the bents
and tussocks, tipped with frost,
turn lank and pale. The ice burns
with clear fire, by day by night.

21

To live with water. To walk over
water meadows, to know the seasons
of change and renewal in the colonies
of water, in the proliferation
of water-crowfoot, the flowering
and seeding of yellow flags; to judge
the heat of summer evenings by the ease
of cattle knee-deep in country
water; to know winter by the stripped
canes of the willow, by the heron's
desperate stillness, the surprise
of ice. To live with water.

22

Boneless reeds betray the stream's
direction. Faults in the quick run,
stones, obstacles, vexing shallows,
all hold back the sticks' tangles, a float
of thick scum. Bright water
hurries under them.

23

Fire, the acid exhalation
of industrial chimneys, serpentine
breeding of highways: the trees
are dead. Where once the natural winter
took the weak, the shallow-rooted,
charred scars mark the paper skin
of the birch tree. The oak is dry.
Their heartwood is soft with fungus.

24

Rampart and wide ditch,
moat and stone keep
lie under the fists
of green bracken.

Barriers of enormous concrete,
long galleries safe from invasion,
all the complexities of defence
are lost to silent moss.

Rust covers the dry guns.

25

Under grass the living rock, sandstone,
or limestone; from earth's making.
However skilled the harsh drill
and set explosions of the quarry,
stone makes its protest, breaking
in unexpected seams of growth,
flaking. Handled in square blocks, ordered
by plumbline and level, it retains
its nature, its silence. It remembers
the seas which made it.

Something happens to a dry wall: the earth
has to accept it. It must be built
with due reverence for the curves and usages
of the land. A field has its own passages,
its underground, differing textures, can direct
the root of trees beneath a wall, point
small creatures into crevices, measuring,
reporting. And if a wall is made wrongly,
arrogantly cuts across the field's
own passages and ways, then a slow,
uplifting, irresistible heave, lasting
many seasons, compounded of cracking frost
and warmth and all growing things, undoes
the wall, breaks its dry bonds, topples it.
Don't think to repair it. Look humbly
at the land, build where the wall belongs.
A field knows its own boundaries.

27

Working with stone, now. There's something
in that. The slow modification
of shape, the chipped squareness of stone
as it takes shape against the blunt hammer,
the chisel. Then fitting the dressed stones
together, moving them those heavy fractions
so they fit, lock well, are solid in the wall.
And then to walk away, tired, knowing
what will happen. That the low stone wall
will weather amicably, accept fern
and lichen, settle into place
as if it grew there. Be a memorial
for all anonymous men who work with stone.

28

Time wears on the flat cliff
its simple messages, cleans them
with rain, with the lunar orderliness
of the sea. Lichen and sopping moss,
those old communities, their growth
too small to measure, their surfaces
velvet on harsh stone, inhabit
the faint declivities. The manner
of the cliff is angular, its lines
clean and direct. It breaks
with a sharp, clear statement.

29

In slum pools at the edge of town,
in stinking hollows where garbage drains
its slimes of drums and rust,
among brittle, lifeless coils
and abandoned car seats,
the dead twigs lie. A film of stones
reflects a faint light.

30

Tight on the gull's bone
this feather held air
in the webs of its rays
and floated the tides
of turning winds.

But ripped from the bird
in its falling death
in the wind of the storm
it winnowed through air
to the still pool.

31

Where shall we rest?
cry stones, whose fate
is to knock about the world,
growing smaller, to fly
from slings and kill giants
while meaning no harm,
to mark boundaries and mileages,
to honour the dead
above their stale bones,
to be silent.

32

Gurgling and chortling
the smack of the tide
about the round
bluff of the cliff
sidles away
with a tumble
of little pebbles
and a wet buss
on the curves
of firm stone.
The plump limbs
of laved bluestone
wait for the work
of the turning moon.

33

Only bones are left
after the tongues of water
have lapped away what was loose
and friable; great bones
of the land and thin stone
fine as shoulder blades. Water
wears at the long orifices
of stone, grinds honeycombs
of entrances into the hard body
of rock, will return, will return.

34

Seawrack and stones in still pools
the sea leaves after it. Fronds
of lax weed the children love
to drag in leathery chains along
the sand, the bones of the skeletal
world when it was made, they
join here in casual pattern we search
for meaning, for significant omens.
But a wind ruffles the water's face.

35

Our scum floats at the edge
of water, a brown froth, drying
on stones. Where a river
falls over weirs, the waste
filth bobs on the tight
waves and sails, a raft
of bubbles, on gasping
water. There's a fascination
in watching our spoilage
float away, as if, for once,
we had become perfectly innocent,
as if the sea had carried away our dirt.
It is a delusion. Our scum
floats at the edge of water, clings
to the stones on the shore.

36

Peninsulas, islands, stretches
and stands of rock,
firm on the seabed.
Out in the bay, an archipelago
of diminishing rocks, unmoving.
It is the water shifts
past such anchored settlements.

37

The conversation of stones is serene
and calm, has polished surfaces
and few empty silences, is concerned
often with weather
and with formal elements.
Stones do not yield, but will
lean harmoniously, one
to the other; are sociable
and fond of company.
Left alone, they are content to meditate,
usually on the possession of solid virtues.

38

On the beach, on ribbed sand
ridged by vanished tides,
among the courses of water
and raised edges of clams,
the boulders lift their animal
heads, and wait. Their gouged
sockets are soft with moss, their hides
scoured by rubbing grit.
Unmoved by the rise
and fall of the sea,
their breathing
is still as marble.

39

The sea carries above it
an enormous sky.
A path, dropping
through bracken and heather,
avoids rocks and running
water, scuttles beneath
dark heights on either side,
turns once upon itself,
and breaks through into the light.
The sea comes up to meet it.

40

Sea-fires cracked Shelley's bones.
He lay on the Pisan shore
and clean flames ate him.
There are worse ends
than suffocating waves of the sea,
a pyre of round stones,
green fires of driftwood.
On the beach, as the year dies,
I light this celebratory fire,
watch the blue smoke, rising.

41

I stand at the land's edge, waiting
for what the tide will bring to me
and what it will take away.

A SEA IN THE DESERT

1

A little sea
 in the night
  ran its inch of tide
 about the bole of the peach tree,

hesitated,
 came fawning to my door,
  cringed,
   fell away.

Its small crests,
 its ebb,
  broke my sleep.

2

A little sea
 was running in the desert.
 It came in
  under the edges of the breeze,
a true sea,
  sharpening the air with salt,
   filling hourly through the night.

It remembered white ships,
 clippers out of China
  freighted with tea and roses,
   sea-swans
 holding gales in their wings,
storms off the coast of fragrant Spain, snarling.

It hurled
against my walls
    its gathering whips and drums,
        dropped away,
its throat rattling with pebbles.

3

I got up,
    opened my door
        to this unbelievable sea.

My yard was lit by silent moonlight.
Parched grasshoppers chirrupped in the ditches.

4

But still the sea broke
    on the beaches of my ears.

My skull was a shell
    holding the noisy tides
Pouring unseen over the desert.

5

A man is moon to his own sea —
he draws it after him,
like a dog it follows him
the days of his life.

All that night I heard the sea make
and ebb, a sea formed
of grains of remembered oceans,
fed by rains and rivers

of days I had finished with.
It carried old sticks in its mouth.
In the morning a tide's detritus,
twigs, small round stones, a can,

lay in uneven lines
on the charred grass.

6

A hermit thrush sings for me
in dry arroyos its liquid note.
I have heard in the desert
unrecognised birds, charmers,

lift up their single whistles,
long separated, distant,
purified by distance, among
the grassless dunes.

I have thought them calling me.
I have heard the voices
of an invisible sea
whispering with boys'

voices, heard in its dry waves
the pattering of boys' feet
through the built canyons
of the past. I have heard

such singing. The mocking-bird
has sung for me. Each day
the waters of that sea
are rising blindly to the full.

DECOYS

for John Davies, of Prestatyn.

1

They work in garages,
in cold sheds behind houses,
in basements under harsh lights,
the men who make decoys.

At desks, or behind
the wheels of trucks,
all day their hands have ached
for this. They eat slowly,

savour their last cups,
and in a dream, breath
masked from the snuff of wood,
go now to set the false birds

free. Their saws are warm
and humming, their burrs
their files, rotate
at an electric wish.

Everywhere is a fur
of dust; of walnut,
of white oak, logged forests
dried for this making.

With the flat of their palms
they measure the neck's right curve
and set with an eye
an angle to the beak.

Such birds must look comfortable.
The glass eyes are inserted
in a parody of safety,
neither wild nor mad.

Now it is the caress
of repetitive fine abrasives
transforms the annual rings
to feathers, to a persuasion of down.

The paint is brilliant,
quick-drying, acrylic,
more accurate than nature.
It is touched with shadows.

There are seven shades of black.

2

Such perfect creatures keep
at the edges of your mind.
They will not breed, are mere
flawless images. Let them bob
in the ebb of your knowledge.

Soon you will forget them.
White-fronts out of Spitzbergen,
flying through sleet cold enough
to freeze the soft tongues in their mouths,
would find your decoys faulty.

Yet you can tease them down
with a sheet of newsprint,
torn like a heart and weighted
with a clod of grass. Set it
blunt end to the wind, and watch

the great birds from the sea
come flighting in. But the best,
the most killing, of all deceits
is a dead bird. Keep the few
unbroken of your last deaths. Place them

pale breasts to the sky, heads
to the wind, and let them lie
on the cold saltings,
on scatterings of snow no whiter
than the fans of their tails.

Do this alone, on a night
no other man would walk in,
wary of ice in your gun-barrels,
the tide shifting, the light
blown all ways of the compass.

You must be still as a dead bird.

3

The gun has its knowledge, its action
fast as instinct. Once, on an empty night,
our sacks still folded, a heavy dew
an hour away with the dawn,
my gun swung in its own smooth curve,
pulling my hands to fire.
There was not a pause.

And the mallard fell out of darkness,
in its weight, its feathered heaviness.
It was a green drake. I took it from the ditch
as its eye faded. By god, said my friend, dancing,
You scraped it off the face of the moon.
I brushed the wing that had pushed night from under it.

It was the gun had known.

4

There are men, they are born with it,
who have the gift of calling.

They live in cottages on the saltings,
or if in villages, move quietly by night.

Nothing changes in their country but they know it;
the angle of a gate, a dropped branch, shifts of the wind.

For them the sky fills with wildfowl. The lines of flight
clamour for them, for them sanderling

and redshank patter at the tide's withdrawing runnels.
They turn, in quiet beds, at a flake of snow.

When they call, when they squat in a hide
or hide in a thick of bush,

they blow through cupped hands
for a meeting of birds and animals.

Call again and again, the note rising,
an elegy for vulnerable creatures,

the hare, the partridge, runners and low fliers.
And for the waterbirds, for rafts of teal,

for pied shelduck, for skeins of geese,
brent goose, snow goose, pinkfoot, Canada,

the little bean goose, hardy in the air,
the royal swan, the whooper,

all humble on land, on their pliable webs.
Let the men put away rapacious lead, let them be still.

The birds have given them the wide, cold sky.
They have given them dreams of innocence.

They have given them voices.